I0505339

The Rise of Generians

How Science is Revolutionizing Life Industries

S. Jay Olshansky, Ph.D.

Chief Scientist and Co-Founder, Lapetus Solutions, Inc.

Professor, School of Public Health

University of Illinois at Chicago

Copyright © 2020 S. Jay Olshansky

All rights reserved.

ISBN: 9798626688368

CONTENTS

Foreword

Most academics live cushy lives. We teach, do research, publish in scientific journals, and then retire after decades of service to our University. This is not the path I've chosen. In the late 1980s I was working at Argonne National Laboratory in Illinois on environmental assessments, but my passion was the field of aging and longevity – which was the basis of my Ph.D. training at the University of Chicago.

On a whim in the late 1980s, I applied for a grant from the National Institute on Aging for a prestigious "K01-Award". These grants are designed to buy five years of protected time for scientists that want to either switch disciplines or obtain training in an area outside of their area of expertise.

I was fortunate to get the K01, and five years later I received another five-year extension called a K02. This meant I had ten years to retrain in other scientific disciplines related to aging while I was in my 30s and 40s, and I did this training while accepting faculty positions in the Department of Internal Medicine at the University of Chicago, and then in the School of Public Health at the University of Illinois at Chicago where I remain today.

The byproduct of this interdisciplinary training was the birth of a new scientific discipline called "Biodemography" that I developed with my good friend and colleague Bruce Carnes who also worked at Argonne. Operating an academic career built on interdisciplinary work is not a recommended path for most. The reason is that most scientists are trained in one area, and they remain in that area for the rest of their careers – often publishing only in scientific journals in their area of expertise. When a scientist crosses over into other scientific disciplines, it then becomes extremely difficult to obtain grant money or publish in scientific journals – these are the life blood and currency of an academic. The reason is that the reviewers or gatekeepers for these lifelines for scientists are often trained in only one area of expertise, so they don't understand the language or background presented by those trying to publish in multiple disciplines at the same time. The frequent result is that papers get rejected, grants don't get funded, and interdisciplinary science goes unrewarded. Welcome to my world – this is by far the most difficult path for a scientist to choose.

The solution to this problem is straightforward if it can be pulled off – find a way to "teach" the reviewers about the value of other scientific perspectives *at the same time and in the same document* being used to try to get funding or get published. This is not an easy task with word and page limits on papers and grants. So how did I do it? Not alone! As it turned out, I was fortunate enough to be working with my friend Bruce who was an extremely sharp scientist that was trained as a biostatistician/ecologist. While neither of us could have pulled off interdisciplinary careers alone, together it was possible.

The reason Bruce and I worked so effectively together is because, by chance, we are both adherents to the adage that, all things being equal, simpler is better. As we wrote papers together, we took the time to explain everything to our readers in language that could be understood by a lay person. If you read any of our scientific papers that use biodemography as a frame of reference – which is most of them – you'll notice that we made a considerable effort to explain everything in clear language.

There is no better example of this than my favorite article I've ever published (co-authored with Bruce and Dr. Bob Butler – the founding director of the National Institute on Aging) – it was entitled "If Humans Were Built to Last" and it first appeared in Scientific American (SCIAM) in 2001. That article has since been republished by SCIAM twice – and it's now recognized as one of the most popular articles ever published by the magazine.

In that article we demonstrated how an understanding of evolutionary biology explains why many of the diseases and disorders associated with aging are byproducts of having inherited a body design that was not intended for long-term use. We then showed the reader what the human body might have looked like if there was a "designer", and if that designer had the goal of producing a human that could live healthier into old age. This paper is now used to teach high school students about evolutionary biology.

Once the basic concepts of biodemography made their way into the scientific literature, it was only a matter of time before various life industries (e.g., insurance and reinsurance companies, actuaries, pension funds, the Social Security Administration, World Health Organization, etc.) began to understand its importance to their businesses. I then started getting invited to meetings across the globe to discuss the future of human longevity within the context of an understanding of biodemography.

This book is intended to briefly chronicle the journey I took from an academic with an interest in the science of aging, to the influence I've had on companies that are now disrupting the way in which various life industries are operating. The irony is that many of the struggles I faced almost 30 years ago when first entering into the morass of interdisciplinary science, are happening all over again as businesses are just now beginning to learn how to leverage the advantages that the scientific study of aging is affording them. Once they come around and understand what is being offered, I expect they'll be jumping at the opportunity in front of them.

Introduction

When someone reaches the age of 70 they're called a Septuagenarian; people between 80 and 90 are called Octogenarians; those living into their 90s are called Nonagenarians; surviving to 100 garners the rare label of Centenarian; and the most coveted label of all is surviving to ages 110 and older – then you get to be called a Super Centenarian. There are only 20 people alive today that can claim the "Super" label and perhaps no more than 50 have ever existed in human history. The other three groups are rising rapidly as a percentage of the total population, and their influence is likely to dominate multiple industries in the coming decades across the globe.

Prior to 1900, survival to these extreme outer regions of the human lifespan was rare, so the last 120 years represents an unprecedented longevity revolution brought forth by public health, advances in medical technology, and learning how to maintain our aging bodies.

Longevity experts at Stanford University refer to the rising importance of this group of older people with such reverence that they suggest entire countries like the United States need to rethink what it means to become older. Surviving past age 70 with regularity has spawned new industries or reshaped those already in existence like health care, work, and retirement and leisure. Experts at Stanford contend a New Map of Life is now required – a way to accommodate the radical changes in our aging world that have already occurred, or which are forthcoming. If people aged 70+ are treated as the only increasing natural resource on earth rather than a burden to society, then we're in for wild ride in this century.

At Lapetus Solutions (a company I cofounded in 2015 with the goal of bringing science and business together) we coined a new term – "Generians" – to describe everyone aged 70+ which is rapidly becoming one of the most influential and well-studied subgroups of the population in human history. While extended survival was rare in the past, entrance into the Generian longevity club is broadening dramatically across the globe.

We changed the spelling from *Gena*rians to *Gene*rians to reflect the importance of genes as an important risk factor influencing the chances of living this long. While upwards of 80 percent of the population in developed nations today are going to live to 70+, how far we make it into this new phase of life is driven largely by the genes inherited from our parents. How healthy we are along the way will be heavily influenced by the lifestyle choices we made in our younger days and the ones we make once entering the Generian clubhouse. No one gets into the club without having won the genetic lottery at birth.

This book is the first of several that will be written by scientists at Lapetus Solutions – many of whom share an expertise in aging biology or its related disciplines.[1] Our first task is to inform you how a group of scientists in the field of aging have been drawn into the world of business and

---

[1] Since we signed Non-Disclosure Agreements (NDAs) with many of the companies we've advised over the years, I've changed some of the details when describing interactions with specific hedge funds or organizations involved in investments involving Generians.

investments that relate to the rapidly rising Generian population. In subsequent publications we'll expand on this theme – illustrating how science is in the process of disrupting multiple industries associated with or influenced by Generians.

For now, let me tell you the story of how my colleagues and I got here in the first place.

I. Investing in Human Longevity

Chapter 1
Hedge Fund Discovers Death

A well-established hedge fund in New York City with a rather famous person running it (let's call him Bob to protect his identity), contacts my colleague (Dr. Bruce Carnes) and I in 2009 about evaluating a group of 45,000 people to let him know when we think they're most likely to die. Bob knew of our research on forecasting mortality from scientific publications, and even heard me speak at a conference on the future of human longevity. Intrigued, Bruce and I fly to New York and sit down at a table in the main conference room of this famous hedge fund. The table was the size and shape of the deck of a yacht. After being served a meal from a full kitchen on the premises – with a personal chef – we finally got down to business.

Following obligatory introductions, we take our usual academic approach when facing circumstances like this – we ask the hedge fund manager to tell us the story of how he created such massive wealth. Bob wasn't interested in wasting time telling us his story, so his answer was brief: "simple, we make wise investments for our clients, which is why we brought you here".

His assistant then tells us about a large bank in New York that created an investment built around estimating how long certain people will live. We have information on 45,000 people of various ages, he said, all from the United States, all of whom have life insurance policies that were sold to an investor in exchange for a percentage of the death benefit. It's an over/under bet essentially. The bank selling the policies makes a prediction about how many deaths will occur each month going forward, and the investor "bets" that the actual number of deaths will be higher or lower than the bank estimate. Simple, right? Bruce and I looked at each other and blurted out the obvious first questions – how did the bank generate their estimate? What were their assumptions? Tell us everything you know, we said.

The assistant placed before us a 3-page brief describing the specifics of the investment, including the assumptions used by the bank to generate their estimates and a brief description of the demographics of the 45,000 people. We didn't know if the brief was created by the bank or the hedge fund, which meant it was possible that data from the bank was filtered (correctly or incorrectly) by folks working at the fund. Regardless, I asked when the forecasts of survival were made by the bank. The assistant indicated these were made recently, and they're applicable to these 45,000 people today and going forward.

After a few minutes reading through the brief, Bruce and I lifted our heads, looked at each other, and said simultaneously: "bet the under". Now this may seem a bit shocking to the uninitiated to mortality/survival analysis, and it certainly was to the hedge fund manager whose head snapped up when we made our declaration in under 5 minutes. He said, "how do you know this?" Simple, I said: "the folks at the bank used a life table that was out-of-date".

Here we were in 2009 looking at a cohort of 45,000 people, and the basis for the bank's threshold for the over/under bet was an unadjusted Valuation Based [Life] Table (VBT) from 2001, which in turn was based on data for the insured population of the U.S. from 3 - 4 years earlier - probably 1998. What they should have used instead, I said, was a more recent table that was adjusted to the most likely conditions present today and adjusted again to some projected annual change in death rates over the next 20 - 30 years.

We could tell from the outset that the overall life expectancy estimates from the bank were too low because we came into the meeting armed with recent life tables in hand. Who did this analysis, we asked? Doesn't matter said the assistant.

Here is where things got interesting. The hedge fund manager was watching the exchange between us and his assistant with intense scrutiny trying to gauge the reliability of the guidance we were providing. We had no idea what the other unnamed people in the room were doing - my guess is that they were just observing, or they might have been the employees responsible for making the investment. There was also a camera on the wall pointed at us with a green light on - we assumed others were watching this exchange from another room. Either way, they all remained silent during our discussion. It was the absolute certainty we exuded that seemed to bother them all.

The issue here is that Bruce and I have been tracking mortality and survival for the U.S. population with vital statistics dating back more than a century, so we already knew that between 1998 and 2008 death rates declined rapidly, and people lived longer as a result. The huge red flag here was obvious to anyone with expertise in survival analysis.

We said, if you use a life table that is out of date by 10 years and apply that to people alive today without appropriate adjustments, you will overestimate mortality significantly (e.g., people will live longer than estimated) because the observed death rates of this 45,000 person cohort **is already lower than what was observed a decade ago. It's a slam dunk we said – fewer people will die than what was predicted by the bank.**

The skeptical hedge fund manager blurted out "what if some of these folks live forever?" They won't, we said, they'll all die. "What if some live to 120 or 130?" It's highly unlikely, we said – the timing of death is predictable and only one person in history has ever lived past age 120. What if a new medical breakthrough occurs; what if we cure heart disease or cancer; what if we replace all of our organs; what about genetic engineering and personalized medicine; what if, what if, what if? – it went on for some time.

We said sure, all of that can happen, but even if it does, unless we find a way to modify the process of aging itself and somehow alter the basic biology of our species, all 45,000 of these people will die out in a predictable way. Have you actually read any of our papers, we asked?

The hedge fund manager said: "I'm not sure I believe you". We said we can't guarantee anything – it's even possible some influenza pandemic could sweep across the country and double the number of deaths every month. He shook his head in agreement. But based on what we see now, fewer people will die each month relative to the threshold set by the bank, and the reason is blatantly obvious – the bank used a life table that was out of date and we're not sure why.

Could we guarantee there would be fewer deaths? Of course not. All we could do is arrive at a conclusion and provide the rationale supporting it. We had no vested interest in convincing the manager to make the investment, but rarely do we see something in the longevity space that is clearer cut than what we interpreted as an error made by the bank offering this investment.

I then asked the manager if he could begin and end the investment any time they wanted, or were they required to adhere to a time schedule set by the bank? We control the timing he said, why do you ask? I said if everyone in the cohort lives in the U.S. and you're going to bet the under, start the investment in the months of March or April and end it in October of the last year of the investment.

If you bet the over, start in November and end in February. Why would we do that the assistant asked? Influenza, we both said emphatically – this virus kills 30,000 – 70,000 people annually in the U.S. Most of those deaths are concentrated in the winter months in the northern hemisphere; it indiscriminately kills the rich and poor alike. Some viruses are more lethal to an older population like Covid-19 that has now been designated a global pandemic.

I then asked whether the bank just reported on the age of each of the 45,000, or did they make their date of birth available to the investor? Why does that matter asked the manager? If the bank's analysis is based on age only, and if you have the ability to cherry pick who among the 45,000 to invest in (we didn't know at the time this was not possible), if you bet the under, all things being equal, heavily weight the investment cohort with people born from October through December.

If you bet the over, weight the investment cohort with people born between January and March. I said if the bank uses age instead of date of birth, then people born at the beginning of a calendar year are biologically older than people born at the end of a calendar year. You might as well take advantage of every possible trick to swing the investment in your favor. A few jaws dropped at this suggestion – they never considered either of these factors.

We eventually learned that Bob chose not to make the investment because of the uncertainty. To Bruce and me, if we had any money to invest, we would have bet the house on the under because the difference in the projected versus known death rates was already known to us. In fact, this was a classic case of "adverse selection" where we had information on survival that the bank apparently didn't have.

Knowing that questions like this would likely come up again in the coming years, and the high probability that we'd run into similar skeptical hedge fund managers in the future, we decided to track during the following calendar year the observed mortality of this investment cohort. We compared the bank's prediction to what actually occurred, and month-by-month estimates we made of the fewer deaths anticipated. The data showing projected and observed number of deaths, by month, were publicly available.

As expected, the actual number of deaths in the year following our meeting was considerably lower than the prediction from the bank. At the end of that year we downloaded the assumptions used to track the survivors going forward from 2010 and found that the bank updated their life tables for anyone new to the investment. *They either discovered their mistake, or new tables had just been published.*

It's possible that the new 2008 VBT tables had yet to be released when the investment first appeared, but it would have been a simple matter for the bank to adjust the 2001 tables to account for the observed changes in death rates already known to have occurred in the prior decade. It's unknown how many investors took advantage of this, but one in particular had the information in their hands and chose not to act on it.

The lesson for us scientists with regard to hedge fund managers was that we should wait more than five minutes to generate our assessment, and when we do so, include all the usual caveats about uncertainty. Truth be told, since that day I've never seen another big red flag like this one; but the next time it happens, perhaps I'll pause a bit longer before providing guidance.

Being Squeamish About Investments in Human Mortality

Before going on, this discussion about betting or investing on the survival and dying out process of your fellow humans may sound cold and calculated, and that's because it is. Insurance companies have been doing this for centuries, and most people with insurance policies experience peace of mind knowing that their loved ones are going to be cared for financially should they die.

Retirement investments are also based on estimates of survival. Some companies face mortality risk (e.g., insurance companies banking on people living longer) while others (e.g., pension funds or government organizations like Social Security) benefit financially when deaths occur earlier than expected. New investments have emerged that allow companies with competing interests to offset their relative risks – it's absolutely brilliant as far as I'm concerned, as long as the investors know something about mortality or seek advice from those who do. The truth is, death occurs with such regularity that if you want an asset class that is about as guaranteed as it gets (notwithstanding hedge fund managers that believe we might live forever), and which is uncorrelated to financial markets, death is guaranteed.

Chapter 2
Another Longevity Investment Emerges

One year after our first encounter with a hedge fund, another hedge fund manager comes along looking for advice on 300 people rather than 45,000. The deal is different this time. Instead of an over/under bet on the number of deaths by month among thousands of people, this investment is an over/under bet on overall survival for a cohort of just 300 people who sold their life insurance policies.

There are several books out on this investment (for example, see The Stoli Worm by Matthew Sheridan; Billion Dollar Blueprint: What Big Banks Don't Want You to Know About Life Settlements by Stephen E. Gardner; An Insider's Guide to Life Settlement Investing by Benjamin Chui; Understanding Life Settlements: Uncovering the Treasures in Unwanted Life Insurance Policies. A Guide for Consumers and Their Advisors by David Isaacson; Life Settlements and Longevity Structures: Pricing and Risk Management by Chaplin and Aspinwall; or Life Markets: Trading Mortality and Longevity Risk with Life Settlements and Linked Securities by Vishaal B. Bhuyan), so I won't go into detail here.

Basically, investors are offering people with life insurance, an immediate payment of cash in exchange for part or all of the death benefit in the policy. For someone who can no longer afford to make the premium payments, or for those who want or need cash while they're alive rather than paying off surviving relatives after they've died, this is a brilliant idea for just about everyone. The policy owner gets cash they would not otherwise have access to while alive; the policy buyer earns a commission; the investor can do well if they make wise choices in choosing which policies to invest in; LE providers make money and employ people generating the assessments; and insurance companies continue to receive premiums.

Driving the investment is an estimate of how long the policy owner is likely to live. Organizations that make such estimates for the life settlement industry are called Life Expectancy (LE) providers. If the policy holders live longer than predicted, the investor loses money, if death occurs earlier than predicted, the investor can make massive profits – especially when the policies are worth millions.

We began our interaction with this hedge fund group with the usual questions. Tell us everything you know about the demographics of these people (e.g., exact date of birth, gender, and anything else you know); then provide us with the estimated LE for each person; and then tell us what was used to generate those estimates. As it turns out, they had a lot of demographic and medical information on these folks, which made our analysis much easier, and they had LE estimates on all of them with some medical history.

The company selling the pool of 300 lives suggested an investor could receive a 13% rate of return on their investment. We told the hedge fund manager we can't comment on the projected rate of return, but we can identify those most likely to live longer or shorter than average based on national vital statistics and personal attributes of individuals in the cohort gleaned from records provided by the bank.

After several weeks of work, we succeeded in constructing a computer program that could ingest all of this demographic and medical information and take into account all of the attributes of these individuals provided by the hedge fund. The result would be an independently validated estimate of LE based on personal attributes that are not normally used in the life settlement world to assess survival prospects, but which have been part of public health assessments of survival for the better part of 50 years. In effect, we created a personalized complete life table for each of the 300 people based on their individual attributes.

The advantage we had as scientists in the field of aging was extensive experience in evaluations just like this. The hedge fund manager was benefitting from decades of science supporting the use of a unique set of attributes of individuals that are highly predictive of survival, and which we had been evaluating for decades. The fact that these attributes were not used in the assessment by the bank that created this portfolio of lives meant we were generating a fresh science-based analysis of an investment they were seriously considering.

The disadvantage we faced (as scientists without all of the possible available information) was "adverse selection"; that is, the company selling the pooled lives or the policy holders themselves were in possession of information relevant to survival, to which we had no access.

Once our analysis was done, we rank ordered the 300 lives from top to bottom with those at the topmost likely to die earlier than the LE estimate provided, and those at the bottom most likely to outlive their estimated duration of life. Our job was to tell the hedge fund manager how many of the 300 we thought would live longer or die earlier than expected. It was their decision on whether or not they would go forth with the investment.

Our conclusion was that if they could cherry pick the top 75 of the 300 cases, they would be maximizing their chances of identifying people likely to die earlier than average; we expected well more than half of the cohort to significantly outlive the estimate provided by the bank. The hedge fund was not allowed to cherry pick from the 300, and so the 13% return on investment seemed unlikely to them – and it even appeared plausible they could lose money.

I don't know whether the hedge fund made this investment, but what I learned is that information is everything and being on the short side of adverse selection (e.g., someone having information that is relevant to an estimate of survival that you don't have access to) is not a good place to be in if you're trying to invest in human mortality and survival.

Bruce and I have subsequently advised a large number of organizations and companies on their assumptions about the future course of longevity – included among them are the governments of Switzerland and the U.K., the United Nations, the World Health Organization, JPMorgan, Prudential, Swiss Reinsurance, Munich Reinsurance, several hedge funds, and countless other companies. I also appear on the speaking circuit for a number of national and international actuarial conferences and wealth management firms because of my expertise in forecasting human longevity. For reasons that will be apparent shortly, this expertise has now made its way directly into the current functioning of the life settlement industry.

Chapter 3
The Ecological Fallacy

I cannot go further with this discussion without addressing the elephant in the room regarding survival analysis. Let's be clear, it is not possible for anyone to predict in advance exactly how long someone will live, and anyone who claims they can should be viewed with a hefty dose of skepticism.

Using population data to forecast survival for an individual sounds, on the surface, to be an example of what is known as the 'ecological fallacy'. This fallacy or error occurs when inferences are inappropriately made about individuals based on inferences about a group to which those individuals belong.

Predicting duration of life for an individual using only generic life tables, without prior knowledge of personal mortality risk and without taking into account the personal attributes of the individual, is in fact an ecological fallacy. Treating all smokers as if they have the exact same higher than normal risk of death is an ecological fallacy; so too is assuming that every person with diabetes that is applying for life insurance is going to face a higher than normal risk of death. Assuming that former smokers who quit 2-3 year ago have the same risk of death as nonsmokers will almost always be just plain wrong – scientific evidence demonstrates that most former smokers carry a higher risk of death for the remainder of their lives than nonsmokers.

The ecological fallacy is not applicable with the survival forecasting platform developed by Lapetus because it is based on a set of personal attributes in people that has been established in advance – for more than 50 years – as documented predictors of survival. While having personal attributes associated with longevity are no guarantee that long life will occur, at the population level, a group of people that possess these attributes will, on average, live longer than those who don't possess them.

The presence of harmful behavioral risk factors such as smoking and obesity are no guarantee that death will occur earlier than average for any given individual, but at the population level, you can take it to the bank that smokers and people with a BMI above 30 will have an average shorter lifespan than a comparable cohort of nonsmokers with a healthy BMI.

The interpretation of a survival estimate for an individual based on population level statistics must be accompanied by an explanation of how to interpret the results. When my colleagues and I provide such estimates, the proper interpretation is that this is how long, on average, a population of people who share these same attributes, would tend to live. *Point estimates of survival should never be interpreted as predictions of the exact age at death for that person.*

Chapter 4
The LISA Conference

Several years after the second hedge fund experience, the president of the Life Insurance Settlement Association (LISA) - Darwin Bayston - was alerted to the work I was doing on longevity and invited me to speak at a conference he organized in Arizona. I had been giving talks like this for the better part of 30 years, so I had a good idea what I wanted to talk about. What I didn't know was the message the attendees wanted to hear; and truth be told, I didn't know the finer details of the life settlement investment either apart from my experience with the hedge funds. But that's not why they were bringing me in - they wanted a fresh look at human longevity, and I was there to provide it.

At the time I had already been working with Dr. Karl Ricanek - the cofounder of Lapetus Solutions, Inc. - on the topic of using the face age of a person to detect whether this could be used as a biomarker for the rate of biological aging. Evidence had emerged indicating that the children of long-lived people almost always looked young for their age during the course of life, and to me this implied that they're living long because they're probably aging at a slower rate. The face has become a reliable window into the speed with which aging is occurring. I proposed to Darwin that during his conference I would run a live evaluation of his face age in front of the audience - in real time. He loved the idea.

This was risky because lots of things can go wrong during a live demonstration. The biggest concern was what to do if

Darwin's face age came in significantly different than his chronological age. If his face age was much higher or lower than his chronological age, everyone would question the validity of the metric - and rightly so of course. If his face age was older, I faced the potential wrath of the head of LISA. This latter issue was not trivial since during a previous live demonstration of calculating the face age of a 32-year-old female reporter from Al Jazeera TV whose face age was estimated to be in the high 30s, she was angry with Karl and I during the entire televised interview.

Darwin's face age came in several years younger than his chronological age during the live demo. He was very pleased with this result; and the audience was amazed at how this new technology can yield insights into longevity not previously considered by anyone in the industry.

Two interesting developments occurred during that conference - both of which were related to my lack of complete knowledge at the time of how the life settlement industry operates. First, recognizing the importance of data in estimating survival, during one of the breaks in the meeting I asked several participants whether anyone had ever created a gold standard life table for the industry that could be used in place of VBT tables created by the Society of Actuaries. After all, why rely on a generic set of life tables based on the mortality experience of insured populations when you can create your own experience tables to drive the estimates for the entire asset class?

Many of the participants were in agreement - especially Phil Loy who was running AVS at the time. He said he would cooperate by providing his company's data - but I was told by several people attending the meeting that a gold standard life table for the industry would never happen. The reason was that LE providers are required by regulators to report on the accuracy of their estimates (known as an actual/expected [A/E] ratio) which is basically how close their estimates of LE are relative to what actually occurs. The methods used to derive estimates of LE are considered highly proprietary to each company, so sharing data could allow someone to demonstrate that one company is performing better or worse than another. Although everyone in the industry would benefit from a gold standard set of life tables, competition got in the way.

The second development occurred during my presentation, and I didn't realize its relevance until later – and it related directly to the A/E reported by the LE providers. I placed an image on the screen showing what the distribution of death looks like for an average group of 60-year-old men in the United States. For reasons that I'll explain later, the timing of death in a cohort like this is highly predictable. However, the conclusion I came to was that the point estimate of LE for a man this age in the U.S. then was about 21.6 years (259.2 months) not taking into consideration any other personal attributes of the individual. However, and this was easy to prove, the chance that a person this age will actually die during his 81st year of life is only about 5 percent; which means the point estimate of LE will be wrong in this instance 95% of the time. This feature of a life table could not be disputed.

That statistic instantly got the attention of everyone in the audience, because the LE providers had claimed to the

THE RISE OF GENERIANS

regulators and their clients that their accuracy rates were over 90%; and sometimes over 95% -- not 5% as I had suggested. How could this be so given that what I told them was irrefutable? I received some rather stern looks from members of the audience, and I think some have still not forgiven me for having revealed this fact about human survival, but I later discovered that accuracy rates in this industry are not based on the accuracy of point estimates; but rather, a window of time for death to occur after the prediction is made (greater than just one year) during which the estimate is considered accurate.

Once people reach extreme old age in their 90s or later, for example, death rates are so high that most deaths occur within just a few years on either side of the estimate. Under these conditions it's hard to be wrong because the shadow of death that defines "accurate" is a range of survival outcomes that cover most of the window of time when death actually does occur, so accuracy rates in this industry **should** be high. I think some in the life settlement industry are skeptical of the A/E ratios reported by the LE providers, but I now believe they're likely to be more accurate than some believe to be the case when using this definition of accuracy.

Chapter 5
Visit with AVS and 21st Services

Following on the heels of the LISA presentation, I arranged for my colleagues and I to visit Phil Loy at AVS in Atlanta. He graciously showed us how their estimates of LE were generated. We sat behind a nurse practitioner sitting in front of a computer screen reviewing medical records in search of key words – observing the entire process from beginning to end.

The premise of how these estimates are done is surprisingly simple. You begin with a person's age and sex, and essentially look up a baseline LE on a VBT table or some proprietary table used by the LE provider. If certain keywords appear in the medical record, or if certain attributes of the individual are observed in the file, then overall mortality for the individual is debited or credited by a given percentage. This credit or debit is called a mortality multiplier. For example, a multiplier of 1.25 implies that the expected risk of death for this individual is anticipated to be 25% higher than the average person this age in the VBT table.

If the people sitting in front of the computer screen performing the assessments all find the same key words on any given person, then internal consistency should result and everyone working at on LE company should come up with the same LE on any given file. This is comforting to the industry at one level, unless of course systematic errors like inaccuracies with mortality multipliers or life tables that are out of date, creep into the process. However, different companies often arrive at different LEs on the same people, even with identical medical records and demographic information. The industry often responds to this variation by averaging the estimates.

Differences in LE estimates for the same case evaluated by different LE providers occur most often because of different company-specific proprietary assumptions or life tables being used, and probably some consistency issues in what the nurse practitioners staring at a computer screen discern from the doctor's scribbles from the medical records. We later visited the folks at 21st Services in Minnesota and discovered that their approach was basically the same as AVS with some nuanced differences, although each company suggested that their approach to estimating LEs was among the best in the business. In the end, they all relied on some form of a generic mortality multiplier to derive the LE.

Following our visit to AVS, Phil Loy was kind enough to send us all of the de-identified data on every life settlement policy they had evaluated up to that time as a way to help us more fully understand the mortality dynamics of life settlement populations. Those data have long since been purged from our computers, but the results of our analysis yielded important insights that we carry with us to this day, and we're enormously grateful to Phil for helping us understand the life settlement industry in ways that would have otherwise been impossible.

II. The Science of Human Longevity

Chapter 6
The Gompertz Law of Mortality?

Why does death occur with such regularity?

When I told Bob the hedge fund manager that everyone in the 45,000 - person investment cohort he was considering investing in was going to die, and that the dying out process would occur in a predictable fashion, I wasn't being glib or trying to impress him. I was revealing to him the byproduct of scientific research dating back more than 200 years where thousands of scientists, standing on the shoulders of those that preceded them, have explored the timing of death in all living things.

My colleague Bruce and I were known in aging circles as having contributed to this knowledge base, but in the short time we had with this hedge fund manager, it was not possible to teach him everything we knew. But I am going to take the time now to illustrate why the timing of death is so predictable.

Let's go back in time to 1825 when the British actuary Benjamin Gompertz was responsible for figuring out what premiums to charge insurance clients based on their age. Gompertz was among the first to devise a formula that quantified the relationship between age and mortality – demonstrating that between the ages of 20 and 85, the risk of death doubles about every 8 years. This formula, or a derivative of it developed by William Makeham some 50 years later, has been used to set premiums for life insurance for nearly 200 years.

When Gompertz discovered the link between age and mortality, he found that it held true no matter what population subgroup or time period he looked at. The data told a common story of consistency in the timing of death, and he concluded from this observation that there must be some "law of mortality" that is akin to Newton's law of gravity that governs this phenomenon.

For the next 125 years, scientists tried to figure out what drove the Gompertz Law, and along the way some scientists that worked with other species discovered that the same age pattern of death applied not to just people, but also to most sexually reproducing species. The Gompertz Law was subsequently elevated to a "Universal Law of Mortality", leading many scientists to search for the biological key that was driving this process.

The key to solving the mystery of the Gompertz Law began right around the time of Charles Darwin in the late 19th century when his contemporary – Alfred Russell Wallace, speculated some 50 years after Gompertz discovered his law of mortality – that death maintains a consistent presence in a species as a way to make room for younger generations. While this explanation for why aging and death occur ended up being wrong, it was Wallace that set into motion the thinking that eventually led to the key that would unlock the Gompertz mystery. It took about 70 years of thinking in evolutionary biology before Sir Peter Medawar and George Martin formulated in the 1950s what is now known as the evolutionary theory of senescence.

Medawar suggested that natural selection does not favor exceptional longevity for everyone because each species need only live long enough to reproduce and ensure the reproductive success of their offspring. Hostile environments favor early reproduction; early reproduction leads to short reproductive windows; and short reproductive windows means a species achieves reproductive success early – so these species tend to live shorter lives.

Less hostile environments lead to delayed reproduction, which in turn leads to slower growth and development; the byproduct of which is longer lives. Medawar believed that the post reproductive period of the lifespan, where most deaths occur in humans today, is a process driven largely by genetic forces – he referred to this time in the lifespan as a "genetic dustbin".

Williams formulated an argument describing the mechanism through which Medawar's dustbin operated – he called it "antagonistic pleiotropy". He suggested that genes that do useful things early in life, such as those that transform a fertilized egg into a reproducing adult, have harmful effects later in life that eventually lead to our demise. Such harmful effects were allowed later in life by mother nature because by the time we reach old age, our genes have already been passed onto the next generation.

Both Medawar and Williams suggested that aging or senescence is an accident of surviving into an age window that is not normally experienced by most species, and that aging as we know it today is an aberration – a byproduct of human ingenuity where living things are protected from the normal hazards of life that tend to kill early.

Neither Williams nor Medawar argued that aging or death is genetically programmed. Instead, aging is an accidental byproduct of operating the machinery of life beyond its 'biological warranty period'. That is, aging is a product of benign neglect rather than purposeful intent.

The key point here is that evolution theory answered the main question asked by Benjamin Gompertz more than 125 years earlier – why is there a universal age pattern of death in humans, and why have other scientists discovered the same age pattern in other shorter - and longer-lived species? The answer can be found in a single word – reproduction.

Duration of life in sexually reproducing species is calibrated to a genetically fixed attribute of that species – the timing of growth and development. This is why a mouse that goes through puberty at 30 days can only live about 3 years under ideal conditions, and why a Greenland shark that goes through puberty at about 150 years can live upwards of 500 years.

This is also the reason why, in humans, women who go through natural menopause in their late 50s tend to live longer than women who go through natural menopause earlier. I'll come back to this issue later.

Death occurs with such regularity within each species because duration of life is calibrated to something that has nothing at all to do with how we live our lives, and that something (the timing of reproduction) is genetically fixed. The "J-shaped" curve we see in humans that Gompertz first observed in 1825 has not changed at all in the last two hundred years, although the curve itself has shifted closer to the x-axis as age-specific death rates declined and life expectancy increased due to advances in public health and modern medicine.

The timing of death for humans is so predictable that I can show you mortality curves that will, with rare exceptions, closely mimic the observed dying out of any population. It was this view that led to our brief answer to the hedge fund manager about not worrying that some in the investment cohort would live forever, for this would violate well-established biological laws of mortality that have been validated across species for decades. There was no way for us to get this point across to the hedge fund manager in the few minutes we had with him.

These observations about constancy in the timing of death led Bruce and I to resurrect the ancient search for the Universal Gompertz Law of Mortality in the early 1990s. Our quest to solve this mystery occurred because of a serendipitous event. I was originally trained as a demographer at the University of Chicago with a background and understanding of the dynamics of human mortality, including a familiarity with the Gompertz law of mortality.

Bruce was a trained biologist and statistician with a background and deep understanding of evolutionary biology. Through a grant I received from the National Institute on Aging, I was granted 75% of my time to expand my horizons and learn about how other scientific disciplines influence our understanding of human longevity. I became a student again, and my plan was to learn how knowledge about evolution biology, epidemiology, biostatistics, and anthropology could enhance my understanding of human longevity.

I began with evolutionary biology, and Bruce directed me to read the work of multiple evolutionary biologists including Stephen J. Gould, Richard Dawkins, Charles Darwin, and yes, Sir Peter Medawar and George Williams. The book by Medawar (An Unsolved Problem of Biology, 1952) and the famous article by Williams ("Pleiotropy, Natural Selection, and the Evolution of Senescence" *Evolution*. 11 (4): 398–411; 1957) hit me like a bolt of lightning because their theories on the evolutionary explanation for why senescence (aging) occurs provided the perfect theoretical background that explained why the Gompertz law of mortality was present.

Gompertz and Medawar/Williams were working on the exact same problem; from entirely different scientific disciplines; some 125 years apart; without knowledge of any of the work completed in the other discipline. It was obvious that no one had connected the dots between these disciplines because most scientists don't venture too far beyond their own graduate training and work experience.

Shortly after reading the book by George Williams, I contacted him in New York and he confirmed that when he wrote his now famous book in the 1950s, he was unaware of the work of Gompertz and the long list of scientists that tried to solve the law of mortality. George was kind enough to write the following blurb for the book that Bruce and I wrote entitled The Quest for Immortality: Science at the Frontiers of Aging (Norton, 2001) ["A skillful presentation of current gerontological facts and ideas, understandable by any literate reader, and well worth reading for anybody who is getting older".]

Chapter 7
Solving the Gompertz Law

This is a long story, so I'm going to be brief, but basically, Bruce and I set out to solve the 175-year-old mystery on the "law of mortality" originally posited by Gompertz. If you want full details, I'm happy to send the reader a copy of the articles we published in the 1980s where we formally presented the solution to the Gompertz Law of Mortality and the full logic and science supporting it.

Basically, what Bruce and I hypothesized was that if there was indeed a law of mortality that applied to most sexually reproducing species, then each species should exhibit a mortality "signature" (a constant set of death rates as a function of age that does not change across time or population subgroup – basically, what Gompertz and others had already discovered). This signature, in turn, should be calibrated to each species' fixed genetic reproductive schedule. Further, if the law is truly universal, then the mortality signatures of different species should overlap once you control for variation in the way in which biological time is experienced.

Raymond Pearl – a famous biologist from John's Hopkins in the early 20th century – was the first to test this idea of scaled time by simply taking the death rates of humans and drosophila (fruit flies) and dividing the mortality schedule of the flies into deciles and overlapping them on the human mortality schedule that was also parsed into deciles. Pearl's experiment failed. In fact, several other scientists tried the same experiment during the 20th century, and they all failed to reveal the universal law of mortality.

Bruce and I discovered why the experiments failed, and the clue lay in comments from one scientist in the 1940s who realized that the death rates he and Pearl used were "contaminated" by causes of death that have nothing to do with aging. When animals kept in captivity die, some of those deaths are caused by events that are unrelated to their biology - these are called "extrinsic" deaths - a topic that Bruce and I had explored in some detail in previous publications. Intrinsic deaths are caused by aging but influenced by inherited and acquired risk factors.

The problem with Pearl's experiment in the early 20th century, and in fact all of the experiments since then, was that many of the animals that died and which were used to generate the comparative mortality signature for different species (including humans), were caused by extrinsic forces. In the animals these included infectious diseases or predation; in humans this included infectious diseases, accidents, homicide, and suicide. We speculated that if this contamination in the death rates for each species could be removed, the "pure" mortality signatures of the different species would overlap when compared on an appropriate time scale - and voila, the proof for Gompertz' universal law of mortality would become visible.

Here is where Bruce and I got lucky again. Bruce was the curator of all of the data from a famous set of experiments in radiation biology conducted at Argonne National Laboratory in Illinois in the decades prior to the 1980s. Both of us worked at Argonne at the time. Bruce knew that there was a group of people that were all autopsied that were linked to the study of radium dial painters; and there were more than a dozen mouse strains and beagle dogs as part of the Argonne experiment that were all necropsied at death by the same expert in animal husbandry – over several decades. It was the control animals in these studies we were interested in. This made it possible to reliably eliminate extrinsic causes of death in multiple species – yielding "pure" intrinsic mortality schedules for the first time. I doubt there was another database in the world at the time that would allow for such an analysis.

What did we find? According to the Figure below, *we successfully generated pure intrinsic mortality schedules of different sexually reproducing species; and they overlapped enough to be statistically indistinguishable once we controlled for time as Pearl tried to do in 1925.* This represented powerful evidence that Gompertz was right in 1825, as were multiple scientists after that, all of whom believed there is a universal law of mortality that governs the timing of death but were unable to prove it.

So, when we told the famous hedge fund manager that the 45,000-person cohort of humans will die out in a predictable way, we had plenty of science backing up that view, but no time to explain it.

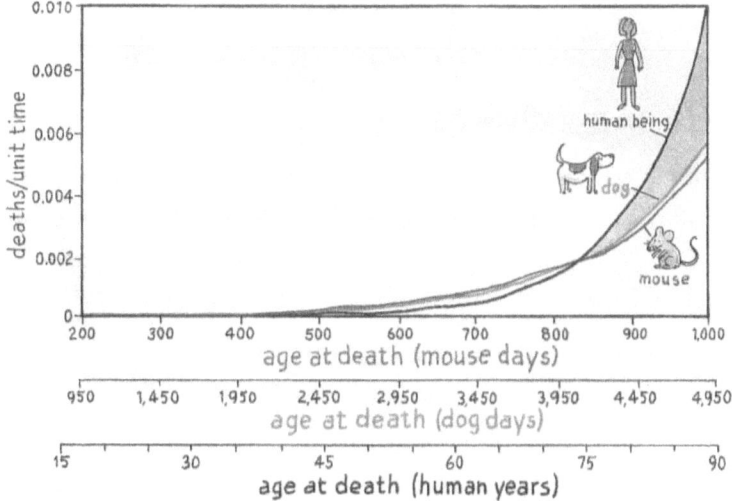

Source: Olshansky, S.J., Carnes, B.A., Grahn, D. 1998. Confronting the boundaries of human longevity. *American Scientist* 86(1):52-61.

Chapter 8
The Birth of Biodemography

Just prior to the publication of our solution to the Gompertz Law, Bruce and I submitted a proposal to the U.S. Social Security Administration in response to a request for proposals to better understand the future of human mortality. It was during this grant work that we laid out the principles of a new scientific discipline called "biodemography". It's rare when scientists are fortunate enough to give birth to a new discipline, but this effort set us on a journey through interdisciplinary science that continues to this day.

At its roots, biodemography is an effort to understand and explain the timing of the dying out process of humans and other sexually reproducing species. The underlying principle is that the mortality curves for humans and other sexually reproducing species is not just an amalgamation of numbers drawn from vital statistics showing death rates at different ages. Gompertz envisioned the presence of something much bigger and more important that was driving this constancy – he believed his formula was akin to the discovery of Newton's Law of Gravity, or much later, Einstein's discovery of the mathematical relationship between energy, mass, and the speed of light. *In other words, there is biology in the numbers used to calculate a life table that actuaries have been working with for centuries, and biodemography arose to understand, explain, and empirically verify the linkages between evolution biology and the consistent patterns of death observed by the actuarial/demographic sciences.*

The field of biodemography is now an accepted field of scientific research across the globe; scientific journals on biodemography emerged; conferences take place every year on biodemography; and entire departments in Universities carry the label of biodemography as do many scientists now working in the various fields that inform the study of human aging – including all of the life scientists now working at Lapetus.

We are proud to have contributed to the modern emergence of this new field of study; and it all came about because of a serendipitous set of events that linked two scientific disciplines separated by more than 125 years. Ironically, it was another set of fortuitous events that led to the rise of Lapetus Solutions.

III. The Rise of Lapetus

Chapter 9
The CEO Roundtables

After the rise of biodemography, our ideas began to make their way into various fields, including that of life insurance. I was subsequently invited to speak at the CEO Roundtable held in Ravello, Italy run by McKinsey. Apparently, these executives heard about this new emerging field and wanted to learn more. Suffice it to say the CEOs were fully engaged in learning more about biodemography and what it means for their business. Upon returning to the States, I was subsequently invited to speak to executives at Prudential so they could learn about the relevance of this new field.

Several years later I was invited again to another McKinsey-sponsored CEO Roundtable - this time in Florence. No one had ever been invited to speak twice at these roundtables; I was honored. A few of the CEOs were still there from the first meeting, but there was considerable turnover at the top. This presentation was also well received, but this time I struck up a strong personal relationship with Bob Benmosche who was the head of AIG at the time.

Benmosche was a no BS kind of leader, and pulled me aside during lunch one day and said he had no prior understanding of the biological factors that drove human mortality, and here he was, the head of a company that was fundamentally driven to profit based on estimating duration of life. We spent a considerable amount of time talking about his home in Croatia; how and why he accepted the difficult position of running AIG and the FU money he required to accept the job as CEO; and his battle with cancer that he knew in advance he was going to lose. With his hand on my shoulder, he looked me in the eye and said, "you need to bring this knowledge of biodemography to our world of life insurance. I'll bring you to Texas to meet with my executives."

The meeting with AIG executives took place later that year, and during that talk I placed up on the screen a photograph of a 100-year-old man and his 70-year-old son – who looked more like he was in his mid-50s. I did this to illustrate the great variability in the risk of death that is present in any genetically heterogeneous population like humans. More importantly, it illustrated the main point I was trying to get across – people age at different rates. Two people born on the same day often experience completely different aging pathways, and some of this difference was due to lifestyle, but some was also due to genetics. This explained, in part, why the Gompertz curve always takes on a J shape with some people destined to die early and others apparently destined to live long.

I stressed that scientists have been in search of biomarkers that can help us determine the rate at which biological aging is occurring – much like a blood test can reveal that certain diseases are brewing in an otherwise healthy body. Other scientists had already published on the value of "face age" as a putative biomarker and documented that people who look young for their age tend to live longer than those who look their age or older. Bob pulled me aside once again and said this was fascinating, and that I should look into finding a way to bring this knowledge to practical use for the life insurance industry. A light bulb had just turned on.

Chapter 10
The Phone Call

I came back to Chicago inspired by Bob's enthusiasm for science and its practical applications. Since I didn't know anything about the study of the human face, I began searching the internet and scouring through research papers on who knew anything about measuring face age. After all, the premise I presented at the AIG meeting was that people who look young for their age tend to live longer; but the published research on this topic so far was not very sophisticated - it involved nurses just looking at photographs of people (some identical twins) to conclude which looked older.

If humans looking at photographs could discern reliably that one person was older/younger or looked older/younger than someone else the same age, surely a computer could be trained to perform this exercise with far greater precision and speed. It didn't take long to discover that Dr. Karl Ricanek from the University of North Carolina at Wilmington was the maven on measuring face age. He ran a face age laboratory at the University; he published on the topic; and was generally considered the father of the field. In fact, it was his work that defined what the characteristics are of average faces during different phases (decades) of life. Perfect!

I called Dr. Ricanek on the phone and told him my story about the meeting with Benmosche and the idea of using face age as a biomarker, but I needed someone who could reliably measure this from a photograph. Ricanek was intrigued; perhaps even energized that someone outside of his area of research was so interested in his work. But Karl indicated that not all is perfect with his work, for he was finding that he could not always get the computer to correctly match the face of the individual to their chronological age. My response was instantaneous – "I don't think there's anything wrong with your computer algorithm – what I think is happening is that you're detecting natural and expected variation in the rate of biological aging. You don't want face age and chronological age to match exactly for every person, because if they did, there would be no variation in the rate of aging," I could "hear" the light bulb switch on in Karl's head. We decided at that moment to begin working together on bringing Benmosche's idea to life.

Chapter 11
Facemyage.com Goes Viral

During a talk I was invited to give at the Age Boom Academy at Columbia University in 2013 with reporters that write on aging, I floated the idea briefly - using the same photographs presented to the folks at AIG - that the face could be a viable biomarker for the rate of biological aging. A reporter from the Washington Post by the name of Tara Bahrampour pulled me aside after the talk, asking if she could do a story on this. I said no - it's not ready for prime time, Karl and I hadn't completed our research yet. Disappointed but persistent, she called about every two months to find out if we were ready for her story, until she finally asked the right question - "what can I write about" she asked. I said why don't we tell you the story of the proposed relationship between face age and survival; the science behind Karl's development of facial analytics; where we are now with our research; and where we think this is all headed.

After discussing the story with her editors, Tara indicated that the Washington Post was going to make this a front-page story in their health section, with pictures, videos, and a deep illustration of the science behind the technology. This was exciting. Karl and I huddled together and saw an opportunity to rapidly advance our research. We thought if we could get Washington Post readers to send us pictures of their faces along with a small amount of demographic information, we might be able to collect useful data that would allow us to complete our research. We decided to create a website that Tara could refer to in the story itself, so we hustled to create something simple. We had about two weeks before Tara was at her deadline when she could no longer make any changes to the story. Our goal? To collect 10,000 images in a year – which was more than enough to accelerate our research.

Karl and I were wracking our brains to come up with a name for the website, when one day at lunch with my daughter Jessica and wife Sara in downtown Chicago I broached the problem in finding an appropriate name. After describing what the story was about, Jessie blurted out – "how about facemyage"? I paused for a second, thought about the dual meaning of the phrase, and quickly wrote it down. It was brilliant. The next day Karl and I agreed to use it, and we set out to create a simple website called facemyage.com

The story appeared in the Washington Post on the 2nd of July 2014, and I quickly learned what the word viral means. Apparently, we had touched a nerve. In exchange for a photograph of someone's face submitted by phone or computer and answers to a few questions, we returned an estimate of a person's face age – that is, how old their face appeared relative to an average established previously during Karl's research. Our servers broke down because of the volume of traffic; we spun up more servers; they broke down; and we kept spinning up more servers to handle the traffic. No need for details here – just perform an Internet search on facemyage.com and you'll find thousands of stories about our site, which gained enormous popularity across the globe. We were even mimicked by Microsoft a year later when they released a similar application. That was flattering.

Within months we collected millions of facial images. The traffic on facemyage.com continued strong for quite some time. What escaped Karl and I was the importance of what we had just done. Within just a few months, phone calls and emails started coming in from people all over the world we didn't know, wanting to find a way to invest in our company. "What company?", we asked. Several potential 'investors' kept repeating the same message to us – "do you have any idea what you just did?" they asked. We said, sure, we collected an enormous amount of data for our research. No, they said, "you just disrupted several major industries all at once – life insurance, health insurance, financial planning, plastic surgery, cosmetics, etc."

Within a year Karl and I created the company everyone was clamoring for; settled on a CEO (a quarterback if you will – Norvell Miller) who knew something about the business world that we were clueless about; agreed to accept over $3 million from an investment firm in Switzerland in exchange for 33% of the company; and we settled on the name Lapetus Solutions for the new company. Lapetus is a modified spelling of the word (iapetus) representing the Greek god of mortality. The symbol we chose to represent our company (see below) illustrates the Gompertzian J-shaped mortality curve passing through the three phases of the human lifespan. Perhaps we need to change this logo because we now think that the rise of Generians represents a rapidly growing 4th phase of the lifespan.

Our goal at Lapetus was simple: help both consumers and the companies we interact with operate with greater efficiency and reliability, and with less friction, using the combined sciences of aging and facial analytics.

Chapter 12
Another LISA Presentation

In the winter of 2018, I was invited once again by Darwin Bayston to give a presentation at the LISA conference in New York City. This time I presented a detailed look into the science underlying facial analytics, and I presented some of my work on biodemography with a focus on upper limits to human longevity and the biology that exists within the life table. I stayed away from estimates of actual/expected calculations. During the breaks and the dinner, I was inundated by people in the industry asking me if I would consider becoming a formal LE provider so they could leverage information coming from aging science to improve their return on investments in life settlements. The attendees at this meeting were enthusiastic about us entering this market, so I came back to Chicago and explored exactly what was required to become certified as an LE provider. Our CEO, Norvell Miller, was intrigued.

After reviewing the certification requirements for the States of Florida and Texas, and discovering that the cost of certification was nominal, this seemed like a perfect fit for us and an ideal use of our technology. After months of work and additional research validating our approach to estimating LEs (the certification process is quite arduous), we submitted our certification documentation to the State of Florida. The folks in Florida were delightful to work with, and it was easy for us as scientists to verify our expertise in this line of work because of the history behind our team of scientists in addressing estimates of survival.

I assembled a team of five Ph.D.s with decades of experience in mortality/survival analysis, and one well-known M.D. with experience as a geriatrician/scientist who has extensive proficiency in longevity assessments, genetics, and end-of-life care for elderly patients. You can learn more about our life settlement team at lapetussolutions.com/team/. All are disciples of the new field of biodemography that Bruce and I created. Our application as a formal LE provider was approved by the State of Florida a year later, and we were just recently certified in the State of Texas.[2]

---

[2] Certification as an LE provider by the States of Florida and Texas is not an endorsement of the LEs generated by Lapetus.

Chapter 13
Lapetus Enters the Life Settlement Market

We decided that the operating philosophy at Lapetus involving the estimation of LEs for the life settlement industry would be simple - generate the most reliable estimate possible based on the application of science to the available information. We would not be influenced by results that anyone wanted to hear nor the LEs provided by other LE providers; we would maintain our distance from both the patient and the client.

The doctors and the scientists would first operate independently, but then come together on each case to ensure a medically and scientifically valid conclusion was reached; and then we committed to getting better and faster at this process as time went on. It was important that we were uninfluenced by the way the industry had operated thus far, and willing to evolve rapidly.

We then asked ourselves what would need to be done to generate the most reliable assessment possible. If we were a patient and wanted to know how much longer we had to live based on our current health status, *who would we go to for answers?*

The answer was blatantly obvious - we would go to an expert that has experience in either diagnosing and treating the particular impairment that was present, or a geriatrician with general expertise in what goes wrong with human bodies as they age. For people nearing the end of life, we would go to specialists with experience in dealing with end of life health issues. We would then combine that medical expertise with the knowledge about population level mortality statistics that comes from the field of biodemography.

That wasn't enough. Now that we had the expertise of the team established, the next task was to create an efficient method of generating LE estimates. We saw how it was done elsewhere and asked ourselves if we could start this process from scratch - which is exactly what we were doing - how would **we** do it? That answer also was obvious:

- everything would be automated, digitized, and done online in a secure environment;
- we would use phone alert systems with doctors on-call and operating 24/7 in various time zones across the globe;
- assessments would include multiple interactions between the physicians and scientists to ensure each was learning from the other and prior experience;
- the doctors would operate in a "hive" environment within which they could learn from the unique expertise each possessed, and get smarter with each review as our internal knowledge and experience database grows each day;
- the doctors would have online access to the latest medical research and all previous reviews completed by Lapetus physicians/scientists associated with every primary impairment identified in every patient;
- A/E estimates will be updated in real time;
- fraud detection and misrepresentation would be built into the review process;

- genetic biomarkers would be made available for use by those companies willing to take a leap into the 21st century of genomics (called the Generian Longevity Panel);
- and every final report would be reviewed internally by a longevity expert before being sent back to the client.

Why Combine the Expertise of Geriatrician/Physician/Scientists and Biodemographers?

Geriatrician/physicians are critical to the review process; in part, because it is often the case that information contained in the medical records drive the estimate of LE. They've been formally trained to understand and treat health issues associated with people that survive to older ages. Patients with health impairments who want to learn about treatment options and survival chances turn to geriatricians for authoritative answers. When a geriatrician/physician is also trained as a scientist in aging biology or biostatistics, they bring the added expertise of knowledge about the latest developments in the field of aging that influence survival.

The non-physician longevity experts at Lapetus have expertise in the following disciplines: actuarial sciences, demography, aging biology, evolution biology, genetics, biostatistics, and public health. All of us are biodemographers with extensive experience in studying the biological and social/behavioral attributes of individuals that dynamically influence survival and health over the life course as individuals age, and all of us serve in various capacities on the editorial boards or reviewers at all of the major medical and public health journals across the globe.

Our team has published hundreds of papers in all of the top science and medical journals, and some of our published research serves as the basis upon which insurance companies have, for many years, been assigning people into different risk pools.

When the expertise of physicians is mixed with the expertise of biodemographers, the recipient of this kind of report is exposed to an authoritative assessment that makes use of all of the various tools of medicine and science to estimate duration of life. We could not think of a more powerful team to put together to generate these assessments, and we believe this is why the States of Florida and Texas were receptive to our approach to generating estimates of LE for the life settlement industry.

Truth be told, our experience in generating survival estimates preceded the existence of life settlements as an investment class, so it was not difficult to demonstrate our ability to perform the assessments required to become an LE provider.

What Is a Summary Adjusted Life Expectancy?

The biodemography team at Lapetus spent years formulating an approach to estimating life expectancy and conditional probabilities of death for individuals that is consistent with methods of risk assessment that have been an established part of public health for more than half a century. The key output is called a "Summary Adjusted Life

Expectancy" or SALE, and it's basically a point estimate of LE that is identical in interpretation to the LEs generated by other providers in the life settlement industry. The online platform created by Lapetus to generate a SALE is called "Chronos".

The underlying premise of SALE is that contained within a base resident complete life table for a national population published based on national vital statistics, are unique mortality dynamics of population subgroups—including the lower death rates commonly exhibited by insured populations and the higher death rates observed among people with harmful inherited or acquired risk factors. These subgroups possess varying mortality risks that, when combined, yield a characteristic generic mortality schedule for a population exactly like that published by the U.S. Social Security Administration, Society of Actuaries, or the Human Mortality Database. The SALE produced by Chronos is designed to reveal subgroup mortality/survival dynamics by utilizing personal attributes of individuals that are gleaned from the medical records.

A base life table for any national population can be used to generate SALE. For reasons I'll explain in a moment, it would be inappropriate to use a VBT table to generate SALE as this would lead to erroneous estimates. Base life tables used by Lapetus come from the Human Mortality Database, Social Security Administration (resident population), and the World Health Organization.

The covariates used to generate a SALE include age; gender; BMI; education; family income; marital status; smoking status; blood pressure; fasting blood sugar; physical activity; family history of longevity; self-reported health; sleep; cholesterol, and age at menopause for women. I hope it is clear by now why we use age at menopause as this attribute is foundational in biodemography as a predictor of longevity. We are certain that this attribute is not being used by either life insurance companies or other LE providers to assess risk.

It would certainly be possible to add in more personal attributes to enhance the predictive power of SALE, and no doubt our team of scientists will constantly weigh the value of doing so as we move forward, but there is a point of diminishing returns where more data about a person no longer yields an improvement in the estimate.

Determining which covariates are the most highly predictive of survival is what we've been doing in public health for more than a half century, so "big data" is nothing new to us. What we've discovered, at least with regard to human health and longevity, is that more data is not better – better data is better. Narrowing down the list of questions – rather than expanding them – without losing predictive power, has been our operating mantra.

The SALE transforms the combined effect of all of the covariates available from the medical records into a single customized estimate of LE — in much the same way that a mortality multiplier is used to adjust VBT base life tables to reflect the mortality/survival effect of possessing an attribute linked to longevity. Many of the covariates used to generate SALE, are also adopted by actuaries to adjust estimates of LE using mortality multipliers. Some of the covariates used by Lapetus are different than those used by other LE providers, but every covariate used by Lapetus has been validated in the scientific literature as an independent powerful predictor of survival and mortality.

The SALE is the first thing that doctors see once they key in the personal attributes of the individual contained within the medical records; but they also have immediate access to estimates of LE from the generic baseline life tables available from the sources listed above. Both of these baseline estimates of LE serve as a frame of reference for the doctors as they begin reviewing the medical records.

Medical Factors that Influence Estimates of LE

Physicians and scientists at Lapetus have gained experience in generating LE assessments during the last year, and we discovered along the way that reviews generally fall into three categories. In Case I reviews, patients are so severely impaired by one or more medical conditions (e.g., heart transplant, stage IV pancreatic cancer, etc.) that other mediating factors considered with the calculation of the SALE are not relevant.

In these instances, depending on the severity of the health condition, the resulting LE estimate is driven entirely by the science supporting the medical review completed by the physician. Conditional survival probabilities sometimes cannot be reliably computed for individuals with severe life-limiting impairments. So far, about 30 percent of the cases reviewed at Lapetus fall into this category.

Case II assessments occur when information contained in the medical records dominate the estimate of LE, but mediating factors are influential in the final assessment. For example, the presence of a strong social support system (especially for older men), such as having a partner or family nearby; high education, strict adherence to treatment regimens, evidence of remission or improvement, etc. can have a beneficial influence on survival for patients with certain manageable health conditions.

On the flip side, the presence of significant challenges caused by lack of education, being a widow, obesity, smoking, allergy to certain medications, etc. can have a powerful negative effect on survival independent of the presence of specific impairments. Conditional survival probabilities are almost always provided for these cases, and the SALE can be influential in these types of assessments. About 50 percent of the cases reviewed at Lapetus fall into this category.

Case III assessments occur when primary impairments listed in the medical record are not significantly influential in the estimate. In these cases, the LE is heavily influenced by the SALE but mediated by information gleaned from the medical records that physicians find relevant to the case. Conditional survival probabilities are always provided for these cases. About 20 percent of the cases reviewed by Lapetus fall into this category.

We don't know if this current distribution of these three types of cases will continue – as much depends on what clients send to us – but every file we've seen so far falls reliably into one of these three categories.

Why Don't we use a debit/credit (+/-) System of

Generating Mortality Multipliers Like the Other LE Providers?

There is more than one way to assess survival prospects for individuals, so don't misinterpret this book, and this section in particular, to mean that our approach to generating LEs is the right way and all others need to change. To the contrary, we see value in taking different approaches to estimating survival and leave it to the buyers of LEs to determine how best to understand and benefit from this variation.

The +/- system used by other LE providers today begins with a VBT table that in itself is a Society of Actuary product designed to represent the observed mortality experience of an insured population. Lower death rates in general are baked into VBT tables because of the well-established fact that insured populations exhibit lower death rates than the general population.

The LE providers then create an internal proprietary playbook or set of rules that link impairments with mortality multipliers; suggesting that people with these impairments are quantitatively at a higher or lower risk of death relative to the baseline VBT table. Sometimes the impairment risks are added together, other times they are not.

When nurse practitioners or physicians reviewing the medical records discover that a patient has a specific impairment, they look up the mortality multiplier(s) associated with that impairment; report that multiplier in the final report; and use it to adjust and generate the final LE.

The advantage of the +/- system is that it should lead to internally consistent results within the company providing LE estimates as different reviewers should always come to the same conclusions about a case if they identify the same impairments in the medical records. Internal consistency can be important to the life settlement industry because bidding or selling policies should be based on a shared understanding of the risk involved.

There is also a logic behind the use of mortality multipliers as they are fundamentally dependent on what the medical/scientific literature tells the underwriters how certain impairments influence the risk of death. In general, the rules governing the mortality adjustments are justifiable. Rules based +/- systems can also, in theory at least, accelerate the review process.

The main disadvantage of the +/- system is that it is generic. Many of the inherited and acquired risk factors that drive duration of life are not measured or used in the analysis; and everyone with the same impairment for a given demographic is expected to experience the exact same mortality rate adjustment.

There is also no accounting for the vast array of inherited and acquired risk factors for survival that accrue in individuals over time and which appear in the medical records; subtle but potentially highly relevant information contained in the medical records may be ignored if a non-physician is reviewing the records (e.g., allergies to certain medications, absence or presence of a social support system; knowledge about new treatments that may be coming online); and there will be no knowledge presented on potentially confounding factors such as advances in biomedical technology that non-scientists may be unaware of.

The Lapetus approach to generating estimates of LE does not rely on the +/- system because we begin with a baseline life table for the entire resident population of the U.S. (or the country of interest); and calculate a highly personalized complete life table from the generic one using attributes of individuals gleaned from the medical record. Our job is to tease out the mortality schedule from the subgroup to which each person belongs.

Chronos is built on some of the same medical and scientific literature used in the +/- system, so the rules governing its operation have been validated through thousands of research studies for the last 50 years. It would be inappropriate to use VBT life tables as the baseline for Chronos because these tables already account for the lower mortality observed in insured populations. Using VBT and then applying Chronos would lead to double counting the lowered mortality risk in this cohort.

Physician Reviews Guided by Chronos Yields Powerful Assessments of LE

The advantage of the Lapetus system using Chronos and the expertise of physicians is that the observed mortality risks and benefits of inherited and acquired risk factors are accounted for directly; unique to each person being evaluated – based on how the scientific literature weights these attributes relative to each other. For example, not all smokers are assumed to have the same higher risk of death as is the case with a rules-based system that treats all smokers the same.

By contrast, Chronos uses attributes of individuals not currently in use either by insurance companies or other LE providers, but which have been shown repeatedly and definitively to be highly predictive of survival (e.g., education, marital status, age at menopause, etc.).

The doctors with expertise in geriatrics or specific diseases add another dimension to the reviews that cannot be obtained with life tables alone as most of the people for whom LEs are generated have some sort of medical impairment.

We don't see any disadvantage to using SALE as the guidance provided is invaluable in the life settlement space, but the use of different physicians can lead to variation in internal consistency. For instance, if you go to your personal physician or a specialist with a significant impairment, you might be inclined to subsequently seek out a second and third opinion of how or whether to proceed with treatment.

Diagnosing and treating diseases is not an exact science, nor is estimating survival with specified impairments, so informed judgment often comes into play when different physicians review the same medical record. For this reason, there may be some variation in the LE estimate depending on the physician reviewing the records, just as you might receive varying advice from doctors from whom you are seeking a second or third opinion for a health condition.

The good news is that we have mechanisms being put in place that are designed, when possible, to channel files with certain primarily impairments listed, directly to a physician that is uniquely trained in that impairment.

We can see why this might create unease in the case of life settlements because of the value of internal consistency when bidding on policies, but our view is that variation in survival estimates from different doctors is an accurate reflection of the uncertainty that accompanies point estimates of LE for individuals.

As a way to maximize internal consistency, when the same person is reviewed more than once at different time periods, there is a mechanism in place designed to channel the medical records previously reviewed by a Lapetus doctor, back to the same doctor that did the original review (along with the original review itself).

Validating Lapetus Technology and Approval by Regulators in Florida and Texas

Lapetus scientists have not previously worked as a licensed LE provider, although we have extensive experience advising companies on life settlement investments. Further, because we have expertise in human longevity and survival estimation, the challenge of validating our methodology was not difficult.

The first challenge was to address the fact that we could not perform A/E of deaths in a life settlement environment because such an assessment first requires that they be made, and then time must pass for deaths to occur relative to expectations. The solution for us was straightforward. Apply Chronos methodology to a population that has been tracked longitudinally for more than 50 years where more than a sufficient number of deaths have occurred in order to calculate A/E.

The data used for this analysis is the most well-established public health data set in the world – the National Health and Nutrition Examination Survey (NHANES) created by the Centers for Disease Control. NHANES is the gold standard for assessing mortality linked to health risks – it is the basis upon which most knowledge about the risks and benefits of health behaviors and genetic risk factors has been established in the medical community. We applied our methodology to early NHANES cohorts for whom enough events have since been recorded.

We then compared the observed ages at death with our projected ages at death using the standards for accuracy defined by the State of Florida Office of Insurance Regulation. The prediction accuracy exceeded the standards for accuracy set by the State of Florida with the use of Chronos alone; the additional information provided by the physicians – which is often instrumental in the assessment – could only improve on these levels of accuracy; which as expected often exceeded 90 - 95%.

This result was not surprising given that thousands of research studies during the last half century have validated every risk factor used by Lapetus scientists to estimate LE in patients with or without primary impairments. The survival estimates generated by the physicians have also been validated in the scientific literature by thousands of other research studies. The very research studies used by Lapetus to assess risk for people with primary impairments are the same as those used by actuaries, medical underwriters, and other LE providers, to generate mortality multipliers used to adjust VBT life tables.

Avoiding Misrepresentation

The State of Florida requires LE providers to have a mechanism in place to identify and minimize potential fraud. There are two main challenges here. First, LE providers have no way of verifying the accuracy and reliability of information provided as part of the LE review, so avoiding misrepresentation must be a shared responsibility between the client and the LE provider. Companies requesting LE reviews from Lapetus sign an agreement that, to the best of their knowledge, the medical records and demographic information is accurate.

The physicians also have an opportunity to identify fraud or misrepresentation, or general problems with the medical record. Lapetus doctors are trained to identify conditions under which information in the medical record makes no logical sense; for example, when the Rx data don't match the impairment being treated. If this happens, the doctor can tick a box during the online review process that halts the review immediately - channeling it back through internal review protocols at Lapetus that lead back to the client to resolve the issue. If the issue is resolved, the clock on the Lapetus review process is reset to day 1 and everything proceeds as before; if not resolved, the review stops, and the client reconsiders what to do with the case.

Chronos also has a mechanism in place to identify

potential fraud. If any of the demographic or personal parameters fall outside of the boundaries of basic logic (e.g., a patient is listed as 130-year-old; the BMI is above 60; height is listed as below three or above 8 feet; etc.), the review stops; the client is alerted to the anomaly; and either resolved or withdrawn.

Going Digital! Life Settlement Reviews Enter the 21st Century

Creating a 100% digital online platform for sending and receiving information regarding life settlement reviews was one of the most important innovations introduced by Lapetus into the life settlement market. The operating DNA of Lapetus is based on artificial intelligence and machine learning since we've constructed accelerated underwriting platforms for insurance companies and organizations requiring rapid and frictionless assessments of healthspan and lifespan using both facial analytics and biodemography. It should therefore come as no surprise that this is the approach we chose when building the internal operations of our life settlement business.

What advantages come with the digital online operations? First is security. Contained within information transmitted for an LE review are personal identifiers on the patients, so the online system for submitting and receiving medical records and the resulting assessment is built for safety.

Second is speed. The moment a request for a review is made, the digital system in place selects a physician for the review and alerts him/her to the presence of a file that is ready for review. The doctor can either accept or reject the request. If rejected, it goes to the next doctor in line. If accepted, the doctor can be reviewing files within seconds after submission by the client.

Third is accuracy. The doctors have instantaneous online access to the most recent medical/scientific literature on the relationship between impairments and survival; access to all previous reviews completed by Lapetus doctors that can be sorted by primary impairment; and importantly, access to the scientific literature used by all Lapetus doctors during all previous reviews to justify their estimates of longevity.

Once a doctor has completed a draft of their review, it is then sent electronically to a biodemography longevity expert at Lapetus for internal review using the same instantaneous phone messaging system designed to communicate with the doctors. Reviewers electronically send their comments back to the physician for final consideration.

The digital environment created by Lapetus for processing life settlement reviews means that the entire procedure from beginning to end can take place in a maximum of 5 business days – our current average turn-a-round time is 48 hours (this will likely increase with volume); and our record from file submission to result sent back to a client is 60 minutes.

Additional benefits of a digital online environment for life settlement reviews include automatic calculation of A/E for Lapetus in general, and by doctor (for internal learning); and the birth of live life tables. If you recall, I once proposed at a LISA meeting to create a gold standard life table for the industry. Since we're collecting our own experience data, we took on this responsibility ourselves and will generate our own experience table going forward. The population at risk of death will be all of the life settlement reviews we complete, and the deaths in this population over time will be the numerators – together they will yield death rates that can be parsed out in great detail based on attributes of individuals collected during the evaluation process.

While it will take years to generate enough data to yield reliable age-sex-specific death rates, it made sense for us to enhance our own predictive power in the future by formulating experience live life tables unique to the industry.

IV. The Future of Life Settlements

The life settlement industry must continue to improve and evolve if it expects to survive in a world where technological advances are occurring at breakneck speed. Innovative methods of operation that were introduced by Lapetus in the last year represent a quantum leap in computing and predictive power, but we're not satisfied – our eyes are definitely on the future. I provide below a glimpse into some of the new technological advances for all life event investments that are on the horizon, or which are already here but yet to be used to their full advantage. Lapetus is directly involved in all of these technological advances, but we're not alone in this quest.

Chapter 14
Genetics and Epigenetics

I am often asked what someone can do today to maximize their chances of living a long life, and the answer is always the same - with tongue in cheek: "choose long lived parents", I say, because if there is one thing we know with certainty, there is a strong genetic component to duration of life. You should know this by now from our brief lesson in biodemography. However, in the world of aging science where we're working hard to intervene in the aging process itself (see Chapter 21 on the longevity dividend), it's important to be able to scientifically measure the effects of putative therapeutic interventions that allow us to age at a slower pace. The holy grail we seek that will allow us to know whether an aging intervention works is the "biomarker" I mentioned earlier - a metric of the rate of biological aging that can be reliably detected and precisely measured in people.

Several biomarkers have been tested in recent years - most prominent among them (in no order of preference) is telomere shortening (the measurable degradation of the endcaps of our DNA which reduce in length in a predictable fashion as cells divide); methylation age (a measure of the rate of change in the epigenome which is involved in gene regulation - a phenomenon that can be altered by inherited and acquired risk factors); and the presence or absence of specific genes associated with longevity and health such as the FOX03 or APOE - both of which are validated powerful predictors of length and quality of life.

In the world of aging biology, these highly sought-after biomarkers represent some of the most powerful predictors of chronological age and our biological rate of aging, and as a result, should eventually become part of the assessment process for various life industries. Right now, most of these biomarkers are most useful for assessing right tail risk (e.g., identifying people most likely to live beyond the average LE for someone of a given age and gender), but they're evolving quickly enough to gain usefulness in identifying the presence of accelerated aging (e.g., an expected earlier death) in otherwise asymptomatic people.

The catch here is that if a buyer of a life settlement obtains information on biological age in a life settlement they're considering buying, the patient will also have access to this same information. Since some behavioral risk factors cause an accelerated rate of aging that can be measured through one or more of these biomarkers, patients might then seek ways to alter their lifestyle and slow their rate of aging. In public health, that is exactly why we're pushing so hard for the development of this holy grail, for it may prove invaluable as a tool used by our personal physicians along with the blood chemistry that is routinely collected before an annual physical.

Asymmetrical information occurs when investors have information that is not known or used by the patient, or if the patient has this information and won't release it to whatever life industry they're interacting with. There are likely to be regulatory issues to deal with regarding genetic information; epigenetic biomarkers so far are not regulated.

Regardless; genes and the epigenome matter, and it's only a matter of time before someone in the life settlement world figures out how to leverage this information in a profitable way, and it could just as easily be both the seller and the buyer of a life insurance policy that profit from the use of genetic and epigenetic information.

Lapetus has already entered this market by creating what we call a Generian Longevity Panel – a suite of genes that we assess that have been documented to be associated with long life. Lapetus scientists can perform this evaluation now by downloading raw genetic data collected through assays already completed by 23andMe – using only saliva. It is already an optional analysis within all LE evaluations now completed by Lapetus scientists, but so far only a handful of companies securing LEs from Lapetus have shown interest in and an understanding of how to use this information.

The hesitancy in using genetics in this industry is understandable given a lack of experience and limited understanding of exactly how to use and interpret the results. My prediction is that some investor will figure out how to leverage this information to their advantage, and once they do, the entire industry will follow suit to keep up with the innovators. Without question, given the importance of genetic and epigenetic information in predicting duration of life, it's only a matter of time before these procedures become critical to both sellers and buyers of life settlement policies.

Chapter 15
Wearable Sensors

Wearable sensors have evolved dramatically just within the last few years, and their impact on life markets is just beginning to emerge. Interest began years ago as step counters entered the market as a way to encourage people to walk a recommended 10,000 steps per day, but the science behind sensors evolved rapidly. It's now possible to track sleep, blood sugar, blood pressure, heart rate, physical movement, overall physical activity, even how much water you drink or whether you smoke cigarettes, etc. in real time. The time will come when genetic biomarkers will also appear as byproducts of wearable sensors.

Insurance companies are already offering more favorable premiums to people that can document that they're runners or otherwise participate in physical activity that signals more favorable behavioral risk factors. It's unclear right now how wearable sensors might be used in the life settlement space, but it's reasonable to expect that in the future when people selling their policies are interviewed in person, the broker collecting data might place a sensor on the wrist of a seller to detect some of the biomarkers previously mentioned – including the genetic and epigenetic markers coming online now. Since personal health information is proprietary and is owned by the individual, informed consent will no doubt become relevant when releasing personal health data.

At Lapetus we already have the capacity to collect wearable sensor data from Fitbits and thousands of other wearable sensors; and download that data to verify self-reported levels of physical activity. In an article we published a couple of years ago in Computer, we suggested that a "health data economy" will soon emerge where people will not only own their health data, they'll have the option of selling it to companies wanting to alert people to products that relate to the messages conveyed by their wearable sensor data.

We envision a time in the near future when wearable sensors integrate into our daily lifestyles as a way to improve health; they'll become central to our annual physicals as this will yield longitudinal biomarker data for the first time; and they'll be used, where legal, in various life industries to accelerate underwriting, verify self-reported information collected remotely; and benefit both the seller and recipient of life products like insurance and life settlements.

Chapter 16
Breathalyzers

In the late 17th century, an English doctor by the name of Thomas Willis was the first physician to describe the detection of a disease using taste – he was able to diagnose diabetes in his patients by literally tasting the sweetness in their urine. A more appealing way to detect diseases emerged in 2016 when a group of scientists in Israel created a breathalyzer that was capable of identifying 17 different diseases using the exhaled breath of patients.

Diseases like lung cancer, irritable bowel syndrome, and multiple sclerosis, among others, could be detected nearly instantaneously – with 86 percent accuracy at the time, just by breathing into a device designed to measure exhaled volatile organic compounds (VOCs) – a technique called volatolomics.

While this technology is still not ready for prime time in the world of disease detection, recent evidence suggests that each type of cancer has its own unique VOC molecular signature. Discriminating between the various types of cancer alone would greatly enhance and accelerate tumor-specific treatment options.

When this technology eventually makes its way to the doctor's office or treatment centers, one can imagine various life industries using breathalyzers to help people (whether healthy or not) identify health risks they might be unaware of, and simultaneously use this information to offer people various life event options like insurance or related products.

Chapter 17
Smelling Disease

Several years ago, a retired nurse in the U.K. by the name of Joy Milne noticed an unusual musty smell on her husband – not the kind associated with poor hygiene. The smell persisted, and some 12 years later her husband was diagnosed with Parkinson's disease. He joined a support group, and Joy came with him to the first meeting – only to discover that everyone in the room had the same smell. Joy discussed her unusual ability with a neurobiologist, who then set out to discover exactly what was being detected.

No need for details here but suffice it to say that there is an oily secretion on our skin and hair (called sebum) that keeps it moist. In people with asymptomatic Parkinson's disease – even at least a decade in advance of the emergence of symptoms – the chemical composition of sebum changes in predictable (and detectable) ways.

What Joy is smelling is a biomarker for Parkinson's, and scientists are now trying to isolate the exact chemicals she can detect and train computers and devices that smell much like humans do, to detect Parkinson's disease early. In similar fashion, beagle dogs can now be trained to smell an intestinal disease in people known as C diff. The accuracy rate for the dogs is close to 100 percent. If you're impressed by this seemingly advanced technology, bear in mind that "smelling diseases" on people was practiced by physicians as early as 400 b.c.

Chapter 18
Optical Character Recognition of Medical Records

In chapter 13 I describe the process by which life settlement assessments are done at Lapetus and other LE providers. A common theme in the industry is the epicenter of this process - medical records that are considered reliable information that is untainted by personal bias because they come directly from the seller's physician(s). These records often come from a time before the policy holder decided to sell their policy, so that information is unlikely to be tainted by patient/physician bias.

In order to initiate the life settlement review process, medical records are provided directly from the physician's office in the exact format originally created. This includes both hand-written notes along with typed information about the patient's health status, disease states, blood chemistry and urinalysis results, and any interpretation by the doctor and recommended treatment options and choices. There is considerable variation in the quality and type of information provided, but in the end, all of it gets channeled directly to someone that must read through it to discern what's important for the assessment.

For LE providers that use nurse practitioners or similar experts with experience reading medical records, the approach is to seek out key words that identify disease states and use those as part of a rules-based system for identifying the mortality multiplier. At Lapetus, unless otherwise

75

requested, medical records are reviewed only by experienced physicians. In both cases, opportunities for errors creep into the review process either because information can be missed when the number of pages to be reviewed is in the hundreds, or when hand-written physician notes are difficult to decipher.

In the future, full medical records will be digitized and optical character recognition (OCR) devices will be used to translate both typed and hand-written notes into their digitized form. Computer programs will be used to identify key words and phrases, test results, patient demographics, treatments, and survival prospects described in the medical record. This information in turn will be automatically summarized for physician review and for use to create the SALE.

Lapetus scientists are currently engaging with companies that developed OCR devices like the one just described, but this technology is not yet ready for prime-time use. The current challenge is that errors of interpretation or omission can be costly in life settlement LE assessments since the information gleaned from the medical records is often critical to the assessment, so the first task is to ensure that such errors are minimized. Once this technology comes online, it will reduce dramatically the time required for a physician to review the medical records.

Some of my colleagues at Lapetus have suggested that it's only a matter of time before we successfully replace physicians with computers that are trained to diagnose diseases and generate LE estimates instantly using information gleaned from the medical records. IBM tried this with their disease diagnosis program called WATSON. This is not ready for prime time yet as the judgment of experienced physicians is hard to replicate in a computer program, but if that ever happens, this industry will experience another radical transformation.

Chapter 19
The Rise and Value of Longitudinal Data

When a policyholder sells their insurance policy in the life settlement market, the buyer often keeps track of the health and survival status of the seller. This helps to more appropriately assess the value of the policy going forward, and it can influence whether the policy eventually enters a secondary market where it's sold again either individually or as part of a package. It is therefore common practice for buyers to maintain frequent contact with the seller – often every 6 months.

What's interesting is that the buyers with frequent contact with sellers are sitting on a potential gold mine of valuable health information, and with rare exceptions, they either don't know what the most valuable health information is to collect beyond more recent medical records, or they don't know how best to make use of the data they're collecting. As a frame of reference, NHANES has been operational since the 1970s; they're famous for collecting longitudinal data on cohorts of people across time periods in the U.S. often spanning decades; and this survey is the basis upon which medicine and public health established linkages between inherited and acquired risk factors and subsequent survival.

At the heart of how NHANES operates is the fact that the same people are being interviewed repeatedly across time (usually in two-year increments) – allowing investigators to understand more fully the factors that contribute to health transitions (both favorable and unfavorable) and ultimately what leads to extended survival or early death. Longitudinal health surveys are the gold standard for helping the public health community more fully understand the dynamics of human survival.

The mechanism of operation after life insurance policies have been bought is to maintain phone contact with the seller about every 6 months. The time period between contact points varies from one company to another, but it is always significantly shorter than the two-year intervals used by NHANES. *What this means is that buyers of life settlements have the option to tap into one the most valuable well-validated resources available in assessing survival prospects and the factors contributing to variation in survival,* **and they don't know how to use this golden opportunity.**

In the future, this industry will evolve to the point where frequent contact with the seller will be used by the buyer as part of a longitudinal health analysis that will greatly enhance their predictive power in assessing survival and the current and future value of the investment. The biodemography team at Lapetus has decades of experience in working with NHANES and all other national health surveys, so it would be straightforward for us to create a mini longitudinal health survey that could be administered over the phone – in a matter of just a few minutes – that buyers could use to their advantage during their frequent contact with the sellers. We haven't formalized this mini health survey yet and illustrated its value to the industry, but it's only a matter of time before we do.

Chapter 20
Facial Analytics

If you recall from chapters 9-10, Bob Benmosche from AIG was intrigued by the observation that people who look young for their age tend to live longer, and that face age appears to be a powerful biomarker for the rate of biological aging. Much like methylation age that may yield a useful signal that diseases are brewing in what look like otherwise healthy bodies, or that biological aging is accelerated in a person that otherwise appears healthy, the face can be used today as a valuable biomarker for various life event industries.

In the case of life settlements, there will come a time when buyers of life insurance policies request a live capture photograph of the seller's face as a way to estimate body mass index (BMI), determine their smoking status (yes, smoking cigarettes writes an unmistakable signature on a person's face – even if they quit years earlier), identify specific disease states that can be detected from the face, and to verify identity. If facial images are collected longitudinally as part of the mini health survey mentioned in the previous chapter, we've now added a powerful new biomarker in the assessment process.

Keep in mind that when blood chemistry changes rapidly in a negative direction (e.g., within a 6-month period as would be detected through a follow-up collection of data from medical records), a signal has just been generated indicating that health status might have taken a turn for the worse. The same holds true for face age – if a swift negative downturn in face age is observed, this could be a signal that health issues are percolating. Insurance and reinsurance companies could use this longitudinal information to help their clients identify and ward off disease and death more effectively, and the life settlement industry could use this information to zero in on a more precise valuation of an existing policy. If health information itself is powerful, then longitudinal health information is orders of magnitude more valuable, especially when points of contact are frequent.

Chapter 21
Pursuing the Longevity Dividend

Life expectancy at birth in the U.S. in 1900 was about 50 years; today it is about 80. Most of this gain in longevity is attributable to declining death rates at younger ages, and in the last half century, death rates have also declined at middle and older ages. While up to 25 percent of the population died in the first year of life in 1900 due mostly to infectious diseases; today, most everyone born will live past age 65. The rise of Generians is a hallmark of success in public health and medicine throughout the developed world, but accompanying this success was an increase in the prevalence of heart disease, cancer, stroke, neurological conditions such as dementia and Alzheimer's disease, and a host of non-fatal disabling conditions. The primary risk factor for what goes wrong with us as we get older is not how we live our lives, but rather, the biological process of aging.

My colleagues and I coined the term "The Longevity Dividend" in 2006 as a way to suggest that the time has arrived to change our relationship with aging and death. Instead of attacking fatal diseases one at a time as if they are all operating independent of each other, a new paradigm of public health has emerged suggesting that the most productive path forward in public health is to attack the seeds of aging itself. I am part of a long and rapidly growing list of people strongly advocating for this sea change in public health, medicine, and scientific research, and this idea has gained enough traction in recent years to draw in billions of investment dollars.

To learn more about the longevity dividend initiative, it's easy to find thousands of stories on this topic by searching the Internet. The reason I bring this up here is that I feel strongly enough about advances that have occurred in recent decades to suggest that a therapeutic intervention that will slow aging will become available in enough time to influence most people alive today. The implications of advances of this kind for all life industries should be self-evident, so I won't spell them out here. What I can say is that Lapetus scientists are right in the middle of this flurry of activity in aging biology. We're knowledgeable about the clinical trials for aging interventions either underway or about to begin; and we bring this knowledge to bear on the tools we've developed that help various life industries operate more profitably.

One example of how this knowledge is now being used, and we expect will be used with greater frequency in the coming years, is worth noting. When insurance companies and the life settlement market identify an individual with diabetes, their survival prospects are debited by a given amount based on what data from NHANES suggest is the life-shortening effect of having this disease. However, the effectiveness of one of the treatments for diabetes – metformin – has now been tracked for decades. The evidence indicates clearly that diabetics taking metformin live longer than non-diabetics. *In other words, a rules-based debit/credit system that treats everyone with diabetes in the exact same way with regard to the anticipated life-shortening effect of this disease, are clearly not attuned to the most recent scientific literature.*

In the life settlement business at Lapetus, physicians are being made aware of advances in aging biology that could influence the subsequent survival of everyone being evaluated; and all of the completed assessments are reviewed internally by experts in longevity science. Clients receiving these reviews from Lapetus are alerted to any special knowledge we possess that can be used to better inform survival assessments. This includes not just clinical trials underway designed to slow aging, but also new medical interventions that may soon come online to treat certain lethal conditions, patient allergies to medications that would otherwise be more effective, etc.

There are a large number of subtle elements contained within medical records that are visible only to the trained eye of physicians – especially those with clinical experience in geriatric medicine – and longevity experts that are familiar with all other non-medical factors that influence duration of life.

V. Concluding Remarks

The hedge fund manager that created a laundry list of reasons why people are going to live much longer than they do now, and why our advice provided in a matter of minutes on the investment he was considering was challenged, indicated that he was skeptical about the investment going into the meeting. I suppose it's wise at one level in that business to be skeptical about everything, but what he failed to do was take the time to learn more about the investment than what his intuition told him. Most of what I explained in this book could have been summarized during that meeting with the hedge fund manager in about an hour. We had the expertise to identify large red flags in that investment; he knew we had that expertise; and yet still remained skeptical about our recommendations.

It should be clear by now that what goes into assessments of health and survival made by scientists with experience in this area, including myself and others at Lapetus, involves us standing on the shoulders of thousands of researchers and scientists before us – each building on a valuable knowledge base. The various life industries out there today – especially life insurance, reinsurance, life settlements, and virtually every industry that in some way is influenced by the rise of the Generian population – would benefit from the guidance provided by physicians and scientists with expertise in human aging, longevity, and medicine. The problem is getting these industries to communicate with each other without all of the jargon – in ways that clearly illustrate the value proposition being offered.

At Lapetus, the scientist and physician teams I've assembled have ventured directly into the world of business. Once we navigate our way through the language barriers, I believe everyone will benefit; the general public that buys and sells life event products; the companies involved in their sale; and the various life markets that have sprung up in recent decades to profit from the trading of longevity and mortality risk. We look forward to helping these industries move forward, and to providing a service that allows for tools developed by scientists to make their way into the hands of everyone that can benefit.

Acknowledgments

While a book like this can be written in a relatively short time, the background work required to create the story took decades of effort. My good friend and colleague – Bruce Carnes – has been there from the beginning of my career, and he's still there providing guidance for me today. None of this could have happened without his influence, so I acknowledge him first and foremost. Other major influencers on my career include Dr. Bernice Neugarten, Dr. Jack Rowe, Dr. Bob Butler, Dr. Christine Cassel, Dr. Len Hayflick, Dr. Jacob Brody, Dr. Evelyn Kitagawa, Dr. Elizabeth Kutza, Dr. Phil Hauser and Dr. Donald Bogue. I'm grateful to Norvell Miller, Dr. Steve Horvath, Cory Zass, and Gary Bennett for reviewing and commenting on this manuscript. My apologies to anyone I forgot to mention. I accept full responsibility for any errors of commission or omission, but the advantage of Amazon publishing is that I can correct errors and republish updates. I'd also like to thank Alyssa Morales for helping me navigate the process of publishing through Amazon.

About the Author

S. Jay Olshansky is co-founder and chief scientist at Lapetus Solutions, Inc., and Professor of Public Health at the University of Illinois at Chicago. Dr. Olshansky received his Ph.D. in Sociology/Demography at the University of Chicago in 1984; he's the first author of The Quest for Immortality: Science at the Frontiers of Aging (Norton, 2001); A Measured Breath of Life (2013); and co-editor of Aging: The Longevity Dividend (Cold Spring Harbor Laboratory Press, 2015). He is on the Board of Directors of the American Federation for Aging Research and was on the Board of Scientific Advisors at PepsiCo. In 2016, Dr. Olshansky was honored with the Donald P. Kent Award from the Gerontological Society of America, the Irving S. Wright Award from the American Federation for Aging Research, and he was named a Next Avenue Influencer in Aging; in 2017 he received the Alvar Svanborg Award and in 2018 he received the Glenn Award from the Glenn Foundation for Medical Research.

Cover Photo

For those interested in the cover photo, this is a bristlecone pine tree – the oldest tree on the planet and one of the longest-lived forms of life on Earth. Some of these trees are thought to be 5,000 years or older. Here is another example.

Photo by Ross Stone on Unsplash

True Generians – a photograph of my parents celebrating their Generian status. The second picture is of my father in his early 90s. Generians are a natural resource we need to appreciate and cultivate.

Abe and Pearl Olshansky

www.ingramcontent.com/pod-product-compliance
Lightning Source LLC
Chambersburg PA
CBHW030949240526
45463CB00016B/2242